Hope & Languish

Hope & Languish

CHENELLE BREMONT

Egret Lake Books

Egret Lake Books
www.egretlakebooks.com

ISBN 978-1-956498-00-4 (paperback) — ISBN 978-1-956498-01-1 (epub)

POE000000   POETRY / General
               POE024000   POETRY / Women Authors

               First Edition
               1 2 3 4 6 7 8 9 10

For G, who inspired me to start writing poetry again. And for my mother, who always encouraged my writing.

Author's Note

After a year of holding my breath, life on pause, I woke up one day and realized I had a book's worth of poems. And they'd been written during a strange period in my life: with ignited love and new friendships, transitions of loss and change, and the experience of a global pandemic.

This is a compilation, an autobiography of sorts. The world as seen through my eyes over the course of one year.

In September 2019, my mother passed away from lung cancer, and I took time off from work. After three months of numbness, I decided to take a big risk and move to another state. In January 2020, I began to interview for jobs in Los Angeles, California. At the end of February I flew out to California and interviewed in person, just as the news of Covid-19 was beginning. I accepted a new position before we fully understood how the world was going to change.

It wouldn't be until May 2020 that I moved to Santa Monica.

A place where I knew only one other person. After two weeks of quarantine, on the first night I could see my boyfriend, riots broke out and lockdowns began.

So much has happened over the past year, and I still have co-workers who ask if I've seen this or that, but then realize I probably have not. No easy way to be a tourist in a city shut down.

Luckily, I've been near the beach, which has filled me with awe and is a staple in my poems. I've also been blessed with a small community of friends who've kept me sane, reaching out just when the isolation became too much.

Despite feeling like a ball suspended in mid-air, I have hope. Hope for the future, hope for my next big thing, hope for love. And if there is one theme throughout my poetry, it is just that—hope.

Contents

Unaware

Heart racing,
blood pumping,
brain scrambling,
for answers to the questions
like a puppet
on a string.
Flailing about to catch the beat.
One wants jazz,
another waltz,
straining for the notes
my hip-hop hips
swing left and right.
Just need one yes
or two
or three.
The control bar tips,
the strings pull,
my feet dance.
Let the right song play
and end this marionette.

February 12, 2020

Inspired by a scene in *The Sound of Music*.

Words
cannot hold all
the regret and sorrow
to erase a sharpened
deflection
cutting a boy
I love

Undeserving
of such treatment
one who is missed
so much

I would give you
all my plums
in the icebox
and wait for you
again

February 4, 2020

I love William Carlos Williams' poem, "This is Just to Say." It's one of the first I remember studying in high school. There is something about the comparison of an apology without regret in his poem that stays with me. This is my nod to it.

Walking in the rain
a wind swept chill

The misty morning scent
of dampened leaves

Imagined hand held day
windshield wipers beating
out a rhythm of their own
ignoring Morrison's Irish
sway

All I long for
is your hand held day

March 7, 2020

Sunshine,
you got the sunshine
all through you.

Let's go babe, out to the sea.
The West Coast is calling me
the beauty is it's free,
it's all free.

Leave behind the newest siege.
Leave behind the confined pleas.
We can take this all the way
down to the bay,
out run it all today.

Sunshine,
you got the sunshine
all through you.

I'll pack up the wine,
you grab the cheese.
Don't you worry, we'll all be fine.
Our world can turn
on a dime
and it's back to doing what we do.

Sunshine,
you got the sunshine

all through you.

I believe you do
let it shine on,
I believe in you.

March 26, 2020

My boyfriend and I would often send favorite songs to each other and talk about the lyrics. I wanted to take a turn at writing lyrics. No idea if someone can take this and turn it into a song, but I'd love to see that happen.

Death comes riding
on the steed called wind,
lingering for hours to steal
our breath.

Plastic red cups
pile on the sand.

Death has always been
near
on the streets
just around the bend,
or laying in wait
in a handshake.

Ten thousand souls gone
each year and never
did we stop
to consider,
never did we stop.

Death creeps up in
decaying us
a wrinkle at a time
until we give up the fight.

And while we armor ourselves
with white thin cotton

or hide behind our walls,

It is larger than one person,
longer than one day,
heavier than gold.

Death will come
we have two options
run headlong towards
or do not run at all.

March 28, 2020

Dismantled bits of memories
keep, sell, give away
boxed up for another day.
Marie Kondo taught
the world how to not hoard
so I've been told.
The only advice that stuck
was to check if something
brought me joy or not.
Do I keep my mother
do I keep my cat
do I keep my silver totem?
Everything else goes.
Except the wine
the wine is good,
at least those rated 4.0.

March 30, 2020

Don't throw away the 4.0 wine! I use an app to rate wine
before purchasing, so I can pretend I'm a wine
connoisseur when I'm not. This poem was written while
sorting through my belongings to prepare for a move. I
also had some items from my mom when she passed.
For certain things, I took pictures to remember them by,
and others I held onto because of the joy. Right now
most of my belongings are in storage until I move to a

larger space. Even items can be missed like missing an old friend.

Compose
our lives.
How do we do it
like the masters
who heard it all in their
head
before they commit it to paper?

Each day an instrument,
individual then combined.
A story told
Peter and the Wolf,
unrequited love turned to death,
or an unforgiving father
a dark and menacing figure.
Each note planned,
an opera for all.

No
we are not masters.
We do not hold it all.
We are mere mortals who
make up each day,
hope for the best
prepare for the worst,
cry or scream or dream
and in the end have composed

our symphony to the Universe.

Date Unknown

I was thinking about how amazing someone like
Wolfgang Amadeus Mozart was to compose a symphony
in his head. To have all those individual instruments
while at the same time considering how they'd play
against and with each other and know what would sound
right. And how our lives are similar, but that it's very few
of us who can keep the whole picture in our head, or
direct our lives like a composer without relying on
technology. Even then, I know for me, I often can get
overwhelmed and wonder, *How did I get here? What will I
do next?* Relationships, jobs, or healthy living—how do
we know what will "sound right," what will resonate
beautifully together? We can't, not until we commit it to
paper.

Flowers are the way
to show your love
when you aren't
there to say the words

Sometimes they are
a way to say you
love yourself

And sometimes
they are just the
thing your cat chews
to annoy you

and then throw up later
to annoy you more

Flowers are unique
just like the person
who picks them

or plants them

or buys them

Sometimes I want
clean white hydrangeas
or bursting yellow-orange roses

or purple and white daisies

They are more than spring
or an apology
or celebration

The world without flowers
is like the world with out

April 3, 2020

I tend to date men who refuse to buy me flowers. I think it's more about their character than about me. Each had their own reasoning for not doing it. But it's still frustrating. I see it as special to have someone care enough to buy a bouquet for me. And while I do buy flowers for myself, I've also had a few good friends surprise me with flowers over the years, and the memories are close to my heart and that does make up for it all.

Languish

The day stretches long
like the sunbeams through
the window
slowly moving across
the room
like my legs and feet
in molasses
stepping across the floor.
Each breath a gift
received   until
        it   isn't.
Who's to know?
There is plenty to do
for someone with
nothing due
lots of finally getting
around to it.
The day stretches long
like the darkness and
the street lamps along
the road
seen only from my window.

April 4, 2020

For the next week
imagine I'm on the Enterprise
(In my apartment)
sailing through the universe.
I'll talk to the captain
over coms or video
(my boyfriend in LA)
Reporting for duty
(to sweep the place, or read a book)
and use the replicator for gizmos
and gadgets
(another miraculous Amazon delivery)
I'll stay in my quarters, a bubble in space
no other human touch.
Next I'll imagine
I'm on Farscape
talking to muppets,
each week a new adventure.
How will you get through it?
What place will you be?

April 6, 2020

Can you tell I'm a Sci-Fi nerd or that I love Star Trek?
Just some of the tricks I used to get through the
loneliness of quarantine. Especially before I moved from
Seattle to Santa Monica. I can still picture my apartment

in Seattle and me sweeping the floor, dancing with the broom.

Day blends into day
the setting sun
announces the night
and right in between
let the bell ring
let each one
raise their curtains
lean out the window
step onto the balcony
and shout out rebelliously
we will meet again
day blends into day
but for a moment
right in between
let the bell ring
and the trumpet sound
with our voices raised
yell or shout or sing
we'll beat this thing
and send our thanks
with all our heart
through clamored
noise echoed loud
to each doctor, nurse,
or front line crowd
let the bell ring
and trumpet sound
we'll meet again

so I believe and
so said The Crown

April 8, 2020

In the streets of Seattle, on the hour in the evening,
everyone would bang pots and yell out, cheering. I rang a
large bell I found among my mother's things after she
had passed. I think she would have been pleased to have
it used so well. This was also written after I listened to
the queen's speech to Britain. She made an impression
and appeared in several of my poems and writings.

Winter waves swell
as seasons pass.

I pace the floor
and hold the phone
to my ear.
We talk of daily
nonsense and
burdens some small,
some great. Some that have left a hole
in our heart. Different but a hole
nonetheless.

Cherry blossoms bloom
blowing in the springtime wind.

You pace the floor and
change the earbud out,
battery dying no match
for our lengthy discourse.
We speak of TV shows, cats, and queens,
or sometimes of our dreams,
with words our only glue.

The summer sun beats down
upon the blue, straw hats and bags
now in favor, beach blankets for picnics
and iced coffee drinks, or white chardonnay.

We pace the floor and wring our hands
will it last this peaceful state
until the fall knocks on our door
and once again we wait and wait.

April 11, 2020

There was a rising worry that while the lockdowns were
helping to curb the number of Covid-19 victims, the fall
season would bring us the flu and more Covid deaths.

Oh joyous day
Cahloo, callay!
Spring sunshine
washes the sidewalk away
Lilies yellow bright
as painted eggs
Oh joyous day
Cahloo, callay!
Cherry blossoms in the air
chocolate baskets built with care
It's time, it's time to celebrate
Jesus rose and saved us
from our sin
Happy Easter

Easter April 12th 2020

I wanted to celebrate Easter and have something positive and joyous written down! Easter used to be a well-celebrated holiday in my family. It makes me think of my mother and my grandmother every year. That side of my family is Greek and we'd often have a Greek meal together.

April 13 to April 17, 2020.

For five days in a row, I drew three random words from an envelope. Then I'd write a poem on the spot and incorporate those three words.

Love not war
kisses not rocks
roll around with me
in the grass
on this sweet sweet Earth

Like a dove who weeps
I walk in sadness.
Sand, rocky, indefinite,
clinging to each step.
What dreams do grains
of sand have?
What greatness
does it strive for?
Am I that grain
along a vast shore?

Sweet little blossom
pink, and white, and black
nothing like the bramble
beside the road.
A breath trap, each spring
not easy on the eyes,
and yet
easy to behold.
Love and hate
happiness too.
I choose the best of these.
Pieces of petals float
in the breeze alone.

LISTEN, ASLEEP, HOLY

Oh silent sleep this city
deep in the quiet of none
the streets are empty and asleep
the shops are boarded up
Listen! there are only the bells
to hear, or pots banging on
the hour
Nothing more.
The birds sing holy songs
but the people are gone
inside to keep us well

Sleek black furred
soft footed purrs
low to the ground
stalking toward his prey
Drips of curiosity
peppered with indifference
and soaked in trust
surrendering to the sunbeam
and belly rubs

Time inverted
obliqueness, a neither this way
or a that
Fleeing through a glass
darkly, a reflection of
what might
nor will
or perchance
Climbing up through the slats
of measured cadence
sweet thick honeysuckle
heavy in expectation
Never moving in
a line, never moving

May 23, 2020

How time often felt.

Waves against
the sand, beating against the
shells and land.
Tiny pearls of rocky bits
smoothing out the roughened edges,
crashing across my memories.
Salty, briny particles dance in
and out, and around the air.
Invisible like love.
Like life.
Like war.
No wait! War is visible.
I hide out at the sea shore,
see shore
buried in sand, and sun, and surf.
Deep breaths, watching dolphins play
in the early morning hours.
Alone and safe.
Sound and safe.
Sandy bits of tiny grits
polishing up my day.

June 15, 2020

The muggy morning
sticky, cool, clinging
overcast skies
Coffee mug in hand
hot steamed milk swirled
with nutty liquid
searching through
posting of apartments
like looking for the Cinderella
with a missing converse.

June 27, 2020

I moved to California at the end of May into a tiny little
apartment. So small it didn't have a kitchen. The fact the
beach was less than half a block, and just across the
street was its most redeeming factor. I thought I would
be there no more than a month or two. I stayed for over
a year. Every time I was annoyed by loud neighbors, or
next-door construction, I'd look at postings for a larger
apartment. The beach was a strong pull, and hard to
compete with. Even the promise of a full kitchen
couldn't lure me.

END OF DAY AT THE BEACH

Last rays of sun
dripping wet in the sea
dolphins dreaming lazily
sand trapped beneath
the toes colder than
a wreath of woes
the gleaming waves
rushing near
wink as if they know
your fear
they laugh and depart
then rush back at you
like a dart
now it's time to go
before the moon does glow

July 29, 2020

I should sleep
close my eyes
and put the phone down.
I should sleep.
At what point
am I allowed to
let go the unrest of the day?
Black Lives Matter
and I don't want to forget
even in my sleep.
Trump is ruthless.
Will my wakeful
sweating unrest,
my scrolling and watchful
eyes upon the screen
hold him back?
I cradle in cupped hands
a friend's tears.
She cries for her daughters
in this ugly world of hate.
I should sleep,
but there is no rest,
no relief. Anger and accusations
will only greet me in the morning.
Woke from the slumber
of before. With much to do
even in the dead of night.
Watching, waiting, doing

Stand up
No time for silence,
No hiding by the side
This too, is Mine to fight.

Date Unknown

1:00 a.m.
News Articles
Covid-19 Numbers
Social Unrest
Political Slander
Stock Market
scroll

.

.

.

.

3:30 a.m.
Email
Facebook
Facebook Videos
5:30 a.m.
Short Video Clips
of Big Bang Theory
scroll

.

.

.

.

.

scroll

.

.

.

.
Tik-Tok
Webtoons
Sleep

teeth grinding
sweaty nights
loud noises
jumpy responses

Doom Scrolling
at its best

August 18, 2020

Hope

The white knight
and the princess frozen in ice
go to rescue
the black dragon (possibly cat...well he has claws and
fangs)
Once upon a time
a long journey was had
riding north along the dusty road
the ice princess brought snacks
and the Knight thought of what music
to keep them occupied
what adventure awaits
it's hard to say, and will be filled in much
later
but they do return and have rescued the sleeping dragon
or napping cat
or whatever tormented vocally crying creature
that hated being on the road was
and then they all lived happily ever after.
The end.

August 9, 2020

With the lockdowns and Covid-19 in full force it wasn't
until three months later that I could go pick up my cat
who was staying with a friend in Seattle. My boyfriend
and I drove fourteen hours from California to Oregon,

then another seven hours the next day to Seattle to pick up my cat, then turn around and back again. The trip was challenging, and we completed the round trip in three days. My cat was motion sick, but was a trooper and didn't complain after the first thirty minutes. He settled in and slept most of the way. I told my boyfriend, either he'd bond with me and my cat, or never speak to us again. I'm glad to say we are still on speaking terms. Both my cat and my boyfriend.

Life is more than these
rumbling noises
seeping through the walls,
or car alarms set to dueling.
Homeless yells,
they are a grain of sand
to make the pearl.
Light streaming through the window
onto the cat curled upon the floor.
Or espresso shots with crème not bitter.
I am afraid the waves crashing onto the sand
will be forgotten and take another picture
and another
and another.
What am I doing here?
What will I be doing here?
This is life
the moments in between,
the rumbling noises.
I could drift through
as if in a dream waiting
to awake.
Or lucid dream
and even in this drifting
steer into the sun
steer into the wave.

March 24, 2021

This too shall pass
the long days stretching out
like death's fingers
the bone-tired grind
of in and after and more.
This too shall pass
the judgment and the joy
of ups and downs
laid out before us like a track
we don't know how to jump.
This too shall pass
even as the days of blue skies
with dips like a hat tipping to the ground
or swooping up and leveling out
our life's work, our pleasure craft
Sleep will come to kiss our brow.

Let us not forget
to slow down and turn the pages of a book
or saunter to the shore,
climb the mountain, perhaps
not to the top, but to a ridge
and breathe in the sharp air.

No more pushing Bitcoin
papers through the system
and bowing down
to the reckless lost

bumping up against the
traitor few who whisper nonsense
to any ear and offer grief
as their main course.

This too shall be left behind.
While we gently lie
and dream of more
and wake to more,
and wish for more than
a society's box.
Shall not hold us
or keep us still.
This too shall be left behind
I promise this, I've made the vow.

So rest in peace and slumber well
sweet tomorrow rushes forth
and meets us now.

April 13, 2021

Alone but not
my phone vibrates
from the text sent
Another State far away
to say
hey are you ok?
A friend after dinner
calls to check
on how the meeting went
even though
it hasn't happened yet.
And through each
thoughtful word
lifting me up
kindness solidified
I hear your voice
everything
will be alright.
The tension in my gut
ebbs away
as my sister calls
at the late hour
exhausted from her long day
just to lend an ear.
I am loved.
All this I carry as my armor
into battle alone but not

April 14, 2021

Tonight is nostalgic
Chatting while walking
Watching the sunset
Ending the evening with a Stoic
Even writing this email to you.

I'm in a strange city.
I don't know what I am doing here.
But it hardly matters.

The buoyant sun
The sinking waves
The elusive dolphins
Bring me magic in unexpected ways.

Time is slow
Syrupy.
Minutes and days drip together
Nothing is how I expected.

I am a little trapped bird
My wings brushing up against the walls.

This pandemic closing in.

There is a time for everything.
A time to sow, a time to weep.
This is a time to take stock,

And not let the noise of the outside world
Distract me.
It is a time to write
A time to become.

Date Unknown

The cacophony of sound
silverware clinking
underneath the rise and fall
of conversation.
The frogs yell loudly
protesting. Or maybe
they are competing
against the horns and
guitars. Insisting
to be known.
Laughter comes in rolling
thunder, and at the end
a birthday song.
Every night the same.
With a rousing clatter of
empty bottles put in bins.
Cars driving off into the night.
Living next to a famous
restaurant has its own
rhythm and living clock.
But when all is silent
And the road bare
The crash of waves
is all I hear.

Date Unknown

During the pandemic there were periods of quiet and stillness. When the restaurants and bars weren't open. Then rules would change and outdoor service was allowed. Then closed again. Then fully opened. Most of my first year in California, whenever it was allowed, a famous restaurant next door kept things lively by renting out the space for special parties after hours. It wouldn't be surprising to hear noisy karaoke, drunken arguments, or celebratory rounds of singing. Some nights I didn't get to sleep until after midnight. My favorite time of year though is when the frogs would arrive and croak loud enough to drown out the rest.

Don't judge me
with your long
line Netflix queue
of vengeful revenge
movies of men
whose dogs, girlfriend,
little girl they were
babysitting got kidnapped
and now all things must die.
You point and laugh
and say, I know how this ends.
This story of the guy likes girl,
guy does something stupid,
girl ends up forgiving guy,
romance.
I know.
It's called Romantic Comedy,
Not Romantic Mystery for a reason, bro.

May 7, 2021

I had spent most of April 2021 watching K-Pop Korean
Dramas on Netflix. One night my deep desire for the
safety of a happily ever after ending reminded me of a
conversation I'd had in the past.

Oh how way leads onto way
And after a time of differential walks
and long over distant talks
we bend both toward each other and away

Can I do it justice
this poem of mine
a tribute to T.S. Eliot's love song

The daylight kisses the rooftops
in the morning time
I with my coffee cup and troubled cat
in my lap
for what may be called a minute
before he jumps away and curls up to sleep

Followed by the sunset's glow telling us to go
as it touches on my cheek
If there is insidious intent I can't find out what
Not in the sky at least

And all the hours in between
with Keto measured bites
and brushing of the teeth
The strolls along the beach
And dumping out of sand before the door
(who wants sand in their shoes—they say)
I know not what to ask

even if an answer were laid at my feet upon the floor

Just you and I, we try again
and speak of things as they were
or paint a picture of the dreams to come
roll in laughter caught by the storm
a vortex, or matrix, or inception it seems

I know them all, the eyes that stare
in the hallways from conference room to conference call
the long whiteboards on the wall
and pens marking out the days

I know the laptops, I know them all
from which the emails come
let us lay to rest these burdens here
and leave them at the parking lot
before heading home in the menagerie along the streets

I grow old, tired, and bare
feel the lengthening of it, the weight
and still I wear the boyfriend jeans (how wild is her hair -
they say)
and my red lipstick (my mother would approve)

There is time for just you and I, for all the thoughts
for a time of napping cats, and brushing of the teeth
A time to revise this piece, and revise again
for us to linger in the twilight of the in-between
even if it stretches us too thin

and if I should go to the shore at last
and look for the mermaids who are said to sing
I do not think they would sing for me
for I am nothing but a lass who daydreams
before the crashing waves, that churn in brackish white
and green
and measures out my days in coffee cups

March 14, 2020

I wrote this at the start of the pandemic, but it is just as
true after. Also, if you haven't read T.S. Elliot's poem
"The Love Song of J. Alfred Prufrock," I recommend it.

We've reached the end.
Of sorts.
Standing in the middle
of the bridge staring towards
the road that leads us
onward to the light.
There.
There is where we
shall all meet and mingle,
each other's elbows
rubbing, swapping air
in gulping, coughing bits.
It's alright.
Herd immunity, or vaccination
life. We'll bump and grind, and sway
in between, exchange the services
or the goods, and laugh as though
nothing changed.
But we are marked. Each with
our own.
The marches, or the madness.
The toilet paper rations.
The loneliness and sadness
in our self-made bastions.
We'll mark it in our eyes
But, we'll keep it from our tone.

May 8, 2021

Acknowledgments

If you've read this far, thank you. I hope you've enjoyed my poems, and have one or two that are your favorite.

A special thanks to G for encouraging me to keep writing poetry, and to then publish it. Also, big thanks to Sandra Rosner, and Doug Walsh who provided invaluable feedback. Thank you to Emy Stecher for mockups on my cover design which brought to life my vision. And lastly thanks to my publisher Tess Jones for not only her professional edits, but walking through this crazy publishing business with me, and having faith in my poems.

And a particular thanks to my buddy who lives with me, and wakes me up at 4:30 a.m. in the morning because he hears the birds. He kept me grounded and made me laugh.

I would say I'm not a poet, but this book seems to say otherwise. Couldn't have done it without everyone's support.

Moving to a new city and changing jobs is scary and

challenging at the best of times, but especially so during a pandemic. Poetry was a way for me to cope.

It's my hope that these poems reflect that we are not alone.

About the Author

Chenelle Bremont lives in the Los Angeles area with her black cat and several dying plants. Before she moved to California, she spent most of her life in Seattle and has a long career in video games. During a two year break from her day job, she learned all about the Hero's Journey and wrote the first book in a fantasy trilogy. After running out of savings (because being a full time author is hard), she went back to working in games. She continues to write in between shipping great titles, and is already planning her next poetry book, several beachside cozy mysteries, and book three of her fantasy trilogy.

You can find out more about her on her blog
Not Quite Jane Austen: **notquitejaneausten.com**
or follow her on **Twitter: ChenelleB**

EgretLakeBooks.com

We are a small, independent publisher.
If you like this book please leave a review on the
platform where you purchased it. You can follow
us to discover more indie books at
Twitter.com/EgretLakeBooks.